This journal is a gift to:

_____

From:

_____

Date:

_____

"I thank God every time
I remember you.
In all my prayers for all of you,
I always pray with joy."

Philippians 1:3-4

Our Life, Our Story

Mother & Daughter Legacy Journal

christian
art gifts®

Our Life, Our Story Together, Celebrating Our Journey

© 2017 Christian Art Gifts, RSA

First edition 2017

Christian Art Gifts Inc., IL, USA

© 2017 Meadow's Edge Group LLC

Editorial development by Stacie Johnson, Meadow's Edge Group LLC

Scripture quotations are taken from the *Holy Bible*, New International Version® NIV®. Copyright © 1973, 1978, 1984, 2011 by International Bible Society. Used by permission of Biblica, Inc.® All rights reserved worldwide.

Scripture quotations are taken from the *Holy Bible*, New Living Translation®, copyright © 1996, 2004, 2007, 2013, 2015 by Tyndale House Foundation. Used by permission of Tyndale House Publishers, Inc., Carol Stream, Illinois 60188. All rights reserved.

Printed in China

ISBN 978-1-4321-1965-2

Contents

1. Introduction

Every mother and daughter have a special story together that is waiting to be told.

A mother and daughter's journey is truly important and is filled with love, laughter, and legacy moments together. These significant moments are shared and passed on from generation to generation.

As the journey continues and life moves on, memories become one's constant companions but more importantly they become personal gifts – gifts meant to be shared with those you love. Gifts that celebrate the enduring bonds of family relationships.

The journey shared in this journal is a special bond between a mother and daughter's life together, representing experiences, moments and memories that shape a legacy to be passed on with the hope that future generations reading your life together will be inspired, encouraged and motived to carry on the tradition to extend their story to future generations.

Enjoy recording your story and life together. There's no other like it!

2. How to use this journal

This journal is organized into different sections of writing experiences, prompted to have you write short answers to more reflected thoughts. With that in mind:

Write a little or a lot.

Some prompts in this journal are meant to be light – even one-word answers. Other prompts invite a little more thought. Jot a few lines or record in a few quick paragraphs. This kind of journal is a bit like an accordion – it can be as compact or expansive as you choose.

Start at the beginning or skip around.

The journal lends itself to free-form. In other words, no set rules on where you start or how often you jump around from section to section. Simply, choose a section you feel like doing, mark the page where you leave off, so you know and if the other person is following with you, they know where you left off as well.

Do it together or separately.

Many parts of this journal can be done in tandem or individually. For other sections, you might want to take turns. Fill in your part, mark the page, and pass it to the other person so she can write a bit. A turn every so often is also fun. But the beauty of it is, there are no set rules and you two can decide how and what is best.

Talk about it or not.

Some things in the journal lend themselves to follow-up conversations. But we also know that talking doesn't always come easily. It's also just fine if you decide to go with the motto, "What goes in the journal stays in the journal" and agree that what you write down is for your two pairs of eyes only. Another way: Decide you'll write follow-up questions in the journal and pass your dialog back and forth. There's plenty of room here for that approach, too.

Fill it in all at once or make it last.

An interactive journal is a perfect pack-along for travel or spending quiet morning or evening times for filling in when having longer timeframes, or alternatively spontaneous moments when wanting to capture quick thoughts. You can also surprise one another with a turn at the journal by passing it to and fro at unusual times and in unusual ways.

Enjoy it twice.

So much of what we record these days is here and now, here and gone. What you write down in a journal, though, is something you have for a lifetime. It's something you can enjoy twice – when you write in it now, and when you revisit it.

Ready, Set, Go!

There is nothing like holding a fresh, empty journal in your hands and wondering what will end up on its pages – nothing, that is, except getting started!

3.
From the Start - welcoming you ...

Mother's Reflections

Highlights of pregnancy...

How we prepared for your arrival...

The day you were born...

_____

_____

_____

_____

The first day at home with you...

_____

_____

_____

_____

The first time I left you with a caretaker...

_____

_____

_____

_____

Daughter's Reflections

My favorite story you tell about me as a baby…

_____

_____

_____

_____

My earliest memory on my own…

_____

_____

_____

_____

What I remember being afraid of when I was little…

_____

_____

_____

What I remember you doing to help me feel safe...

_____

_____

_____

_____

_____

_____

_____

Things I remember about where we lived when I was young...

_____

_____

_____

_____

_____

_____

_____

Mother's Reflections

What I remember about the beginning with you...

Bath time...

_____

_____

_____

Eating...

_____

_____

_____

Laughter...

_____

_____

_____

First words...

_____

_____

_____

Potty training...

Crawling and walking...

Achieving something...

Toys...

Haircuts and styles...

Boo-boos and bruises...

Daughter's Reflections

My earliest memory about things...

Bath time...

_____

_____

_____

Eating...

_____

_____

_____

Laughter...

_____

_____

_____

Talking...

_____

_____

Potty training...

_____

_____

Crawling and walking...

_____

_____

Achieving something...

_____

_____

Toys...

_____

_____

My hairstyle...

_____

_____

Boo-boos and bruises...

_____

_____

The LORD has done
great things for us, and we
are filled with joy.

Psalm 126:3

4.
Favorites - there are
so many!

Mother's Favorites - there are so many!

1. Holiday...

2. Season...

3. Color...

4. Scent...

5. Song...

6. Book...

7. Meal...

8. Drink...

9. Dessert...

10. Day of the week...

_____

11. Flower...

_____

12. Pet...

_____

13. Animal...

_____

14. Quote...

_____

15. Weather...

_____

16. Author...

_____

17. Singer...

_____

18. Actor/Actress...

_____

Daughter's Favorites - there are so many!

1. Holiday...

2. Season...

3. Color...

4. Scent...

5. Song...

6. Book...

7. Meal...

8. Drink...

9. Dessert...

10. Day of the week...

_____

11. Flower...

_____

12. Pet...

_____

13. Animal...

_____

14. Quote...

_____

15. Weather...

_____

16. Author...

_____

17. Singer...

_____

18. Actor/Actress...

_____

More of Mother's Favorites

19. President...

20. Superhero...

21. Princess...

22. Music genre...

23. Drama...

24. Action movie...

25. Comedy movie...

26. Scary movie...

27. TV show...

28. Website...

29. App...

30. Game...

31. Sport/Activity...

32. Sports team...

33. Vacation spot...

34. Things about my daughter...

More of Daughter's Favorites

19. President...

20. Superhero...

21. Princess...

22. Music genre...

23. Drama...

24. Action movie...

25. Comedy movie...

26. Scary movie...

27. TV show…

_____

28. Website…

_____

29. App…

_____

30. Game…

_____

31. Sport/Activity…

_____

32. Sports team…

_____

33. Vacation spot…

_____

34. Things about my mother…

_____

_____

_____

Mother's Not-So-Favorite Things

Some of my pet peeves are...

_____

_____

_____

_____

_____

A few habits I wish I could break...

_____

_____

_____

_____

_____

The worst food I've ever had...

_____

_____

_____

_____

My least favorite chore...

_____

_____

_____

_____

The worst movie I have ever seen...

_____

_____

_____

_____

The one thing that I wish I could change about life...

_____

_____

_____

_____

Daughter's Not-So-Favorite Things

Some of my pet peeves are…

_____

_____

_____

_____

_____

A few habits I wish I could break…

_____

_____

_____

_____

_____

The worst food I've ever had…

_____

_____

_____

_____

My least favorite chore...

_____

_____

_____

_____

_____

The worst movie I have ever seen...

_____

_____

_____

_____

The one thing that I wish I could change about life...

_____

_____

_____

_____

Thank You for making me
so wonderfully complex!
Your workmanship is marvelous –
how well I know it.

Psalm 139:14

5.
Similarities
and Differences -
who we are

Mother's Reflections
What we have in common...

Physical appearance...

_____

_____

_____

_____

_____

_____

Actions and thoughts...

_____

_____

_____

_____

_____

_____

Ways we are different...

Physical appearance...

_____

_____

_____

_____

_____

Actions and thoughts...

_____

_____

_____

_____

What I appreciate most about who you are...

_____

_____

_____

_____

Daughter's Reflections
What we have in common...

Physical appearance...

_____

_____

_____

_____

_____

Actions and thoughts...

_____

_____

_____

_____

_____

Ways we are different...

Physical appearance...

_____

_____

_____

_____

_____

Actions and thoughts...

_____

_____

_____

_____

_____

What I appreciate most about who you are...

_____

_____

_____

_____

You saw me before I was born.
Every day of my life was recorded
in Your book. Every moment was laid
out before a single day had passed.

Psalm 139:16

6.
Firsts - history
in the making

Mother's Firsts - history in the making

1. Pet...

2. Trip...

3. Time to play in the snow or swim in water...

4. School...

5. Teacher...

6. Friend...

7. Sleepover...

8. Crush...

9. Boyfriend...

10. Kiss...

11. Sport I played...

12. Coach...

13. Club I participated in...

14. Musical instrument I played...

15. Academic award...

16. Athletic award...

17. Other award...

18. Job...

19. Day of college...

Daughter's Firsts - history in the making

1. Pet...

2. Trip...

3. Time to play in the snow or swim in water...

4. School...

5. Teacher...

6. Friend...

7. Sleepover...

8. Crush...

9. Boyfriend...

10. Kiss...

11. Sport I played...

12. Coach...

13. Club I participated in...

14. Musical instrument I played...

15. Academic award...

16. Athletic award...

17. Other award...

18. Job...

19. Day of College...

We are God's masterpiece.
He has created us anew in
Christ Jesus, so we can do
the good things He
planned for us long ago.

Ephesians 2:10

7.
Handprints - making our mark!

Mother's Handprints - making our mark!

Draw an outline of your hand on this page. Be creative and color, write or draw inside of it to show what's on your mind and heart at this point in your life. Date _____

Daughter's Handprints - making our mark!

Draw an outline of your hand on this page. Be creative and color, write or draw inside of it to show what's on your mind and heart at this point in your life. Date _____

Gracious words are
a honeycomb, sweet to the soul
and healing to the bones.

Proverbs 16:24

8.
Letters -
a personal note

To My Daughter,

What I like most about you...

All the things you do for me for which I am thankful...

To My Mother,

What I like most about you...

All the things you do for me for which I am thankful...

To My Daughter,

A funny story about me before you were born...

To My Mother,

A funny story about me that you should know...

To My Daughter,

Here is a list of all the things that I would love to do with you before you get married...

The most fun thing that I remember doing with you is…

To My Mother,

Here is a list of all the things that I would love to do with you before I graduate high school...

The most fun thing that I remember doing with you is...

To My Daughter,

My most favorite memory before you went to kindergarten is...

My most favorite memory of you in elementary school is...

My most favorite memory of you as a teenager is...

To My Mother,

My most favorite memory together before kindergarten is...

My most favorite memory together during elementary school is...

My most favorite memory together during my teen years is...

To My Daughter,

Date _____

Where I see you in 5 years...

Where I see you in 10 years...

Where I see you in 15 years...

To My Mother,

Date _____

Where I see you in 5 years...

Where I see you in 10 years...

Where I see you in 15 years...

To My Daughter,

When you meet that special guy, please remember...

The first time I met your father...

To My Mother,

What I have learned from you about loving relationships and how I plan to apply that to the man I marry...

When I meet "the one," here's what I am looking for in him...

To My Daughter,

Some of my most embarrassing moments and how I handled them...

To My Mother,

Some of my most embarrassing moments and how I handled them...

To My Daughter,

What I love and don't love about all the talks we have...

To My Mother,

What I love and don't love about all the talks we have…

To My Daughter,

When you grow up, the thing that I will miss most about you is...

The tradition that I hope you continue doing with your family in the future is...

To My Mother,

When I grow up, the thing that I will miss most about you is...

The tradition that I will continue with my family in the future is...

To My Daughter,

This is my testimony about my faith...

To My Mother,

This is my testimony about my faith...

"I know the plans I have for you,"
declares the LORD, "plans to prosper you
and not to harm you, plans to
give you hope and a future."

Jeremiah 29:11

9.
Hopes and Dreams –
where we are going...

Mother's Hopes and Dreams

If I could travel anywhere...

_____

_____

_____

_____

If I could buy anything...

_____

_____

_____

_____

If I could meet anyone...

_____

_____

_____

_____

If I could be anything...

_____

_____

_____

_____

_____

_____

_____

If I could say anything...

_____

_____

_____

_____

_____

_____

_____

_____

Daughter's Hopes and Dreams

If I could travel anywhere...

_____

_____

_____

_____

If I could buy anything...

_____

_____

_____

_____

If I could meet anyone...

_____

_____

_____

_____

If I could be anything…

If I could say anything…

Mother's Hopes and Dreams

If I had a million dollars...

_____

_____

_____

_____

_____

If I could influence the president...

_____

_____

_____

If I could live anywhere...

_____

_____

_____

_____

If I could change anything...

If I had 3 wishes, they would be...

1).

2).

3).

Daughter's Hopes and Dreams

If I had a million dollars…

_____

_____

_____

_____

_____

If I could influence the president…

_____

_____

_____

_____

If I could live anywhere…

_____

_____

_____

_____

If I could change anything...

_____

_____

_____

_____

_____

If I had 3 wishes, they would be...

1). _____

_____

2). _____

_____

3). _____

_____

_____

Mother's Hopes and Dreams

Hopes/dreams I have about your wedding day...

Hopes/dreams I have about your future...

_____

_____

_____

_____

_____

_____

_____

_____

What I wanted to be "when I grew up" and why I am
thankful for what I am today...

_____

_____

_____

_____

_____

_____

Daughter's Hopes and Dreams

Hopes/dreams I have about my wedding day...

Hopes/dreams I have about my future...

_____

_____

_____

_____

_____

_____

_____

_____

What I want to be "when I grow up" and why...

_____

_____

_____

_____

_____

Mother's Hopes and Dreams

If there were no consequences, then I would...

If I could make a movie into real life, I would choose...

_____

_____

_____

_____

My hope for my future is...

_____

_____

_____

_____

_____

_____

_____

_____

_____

_____

Daughter's Hopes and Dreams

If there were no consequences, then I would…

If I could make a movie into real life, I would choose...

_____

_____

_____

_____

My hope for your future is...

_____

_____

_____

_____

_____

_____

_____

_____

_____

_____

_____

Love each other deeply
with all your heart.

1 Peter 1:22

10.
Time Together -
moments that
matter most!

Time Together - moments that matter most!

As your mother...

My favorite thing to do with you is...

Some things that I would love for us to do together...

Time Together - moments that matter most!
As your daughter...

My favorite thing to do with you is...

Some things that I would love for us to do together...

Time Together - moments that matter most!

As your mother...

Three of my top memories with you are...

1). _____

_____

_____

_____

_____

2). _____

_____

_____

_____

_____

3). _____

_____

_____

_____

_____

Some hard times we have shared and survived together...

Time Together - moments that matter most!
As your daughter...

Three of my top memories with you are...

1). _____

_____

_____

_____

_____

2). _____

_____

_____

_____

_____

3). _____

_____

_____

_____

_____

Some hard times we have shared and survived together...

As iron sharpens iron,
so a friend sharpens a friend.

Proverbs 27:17

11.
Friendships - wisdom in relationships

Friendships – wisdom in relationships

Mother's Reflections

My first best friend was _____

Why we were friends and what I remember about her...

_____

_____

_____

_____

_____

_____

_____

_____

_____

_____

_____

_____

My best friend today is _____ .

Why we are friends and what I learn from her...

_____

_____

_____

_____

_____

_____

_____

_____

_____

_____

_____

_____

_____

Friendships – wisdom in relationships

Daughter's Reflections

My first best friend was _____

Why we were friends and what I remember about her...

_____

_____

_____

_____

_____

_____

_____

_____

_____

_____

_____

_____

_____

_____

My best friend today is _____

Why we are friends and what I learn from her...

_____

_____

_____

_____

_____

_____

_____

_____

_____

_____

_____

_____

_____

_____

_____

_____

_____

_____

_____

Friendships – wisdom in relationships

Mother's Wisdom

My best advice regarding choosing friends...

My best advice about how to be a good friend...

Friendships – wisdom in relationships

Daughter's Wisdom

What I have learned about friendship so far…

What I still want to know about friendship...

This is the day the Lᴏʀᴅ has made.
We will rejoice and be glad in it.

Psalm 118:24

12.
Monthly Diary -
experiences together
through the year...

Mother's Monthly Diary –

experiences together through the year...

Instructions – make a journal entry for each month. Date it with the year you make the entry. For example, you might write January's journal entry in a different year than you record October's journal entry.

JANUARY

_____

_____

_____

_____

_____

FEBRUARY

_____

_____

_____

_____

_____

MARCH

APRIL

Daughter's Monthly Diary –

experiences together through the year...

Instructions – make a journal entry for each month. Date it with the year you make the entry. For example, you might write January's journal entry in a different year than you record October's journal entry.

JANUARY

FEBRUARY

MARCH

APRIL

Mother's Monthly Diary –
experiences together through the year...

MAY

_____

_____

_____

JUNE

_____

_____

_____

_____

JULY

_____

_____

_____

_____

AUGUST

SEPTEMBER

Daughter's Monthly Diary –
experiences together through the year...

MAY

_____
_____
_____

JUNE

_____
_____
_____
_____
_____

JULY

_____
_____
_____
_____

AUGUST

SEPTEMBER

Mother's Monthly Diary -
experiences together through the year...

OCTOBER

NOVEMBER

DECEMBER

_____

_____

_____

_____

_____

_____

_____

OTHER DIARY NOTES

_____

_____

_____

_____

_____

_____

_____

Daughter's Monthly Diary -
experiences together through the year...

OCTOBER

_____

_____

_____

_____

_____

NOVEMBER

_____

_____

_____

_____

_____

_____

_____

DECEMBER

OTHER DIARY NOTES

Give thanks to the LORD,
for He is good! His faithful
love endures forever.

Psalm 107:1

13.
Events - etched in our memories!

Mother's Events - etched in our memories!

Your first day of preschool...

_____

_____

Your first day of kindergarten...

_____

_____

Your first day of middle school...

_____

_____

Your first day of high school...

_____

_____

Your first role in acting (play, theater, drama)...

_____

_____

_____

The first boy you liked...

_____

_____

Your first date...

_____

_____

Your first dance...

_____

_____

Your first prom or banquet...

_____

_____

The day you gave your life to God...

_____

_____

_____

_____

Daughter's Events - etched in our memories!

My first day of preschool...

_____

_____

My first day of kindergarten...

_____

_____

My first day of middle school...

_____

_____

My first day of high school...

_____

_____

My first role in acting (play, theater, drama)...

_____

_____

The first boy I liked...

_____

_____

My first date...

_____

_____

My first dance...

_____

_____

My first prom or banquet...

_____

_____

The day I gave my life to God...

_____

_____

_____

_____

Mother's Events - etched in our memories!

Notes about your senior year...

Pictures...

_____

_____

_____

_____

_____

Homecoming...

_____

_____

_____

_____

Prom...

_____

_____

_____

_____

Parties...

_____

_____

_____

_____

Graduation...

_____

_____

_____

_____

Graduation gifts...

_____

_____

_____

Jobs...

_____

_____

_____

Daughter's Events - etched in our memories!
Notes about my senior year...

Pictures...

_____

_____

_____

_____

Homecoming...

_____

_____

_____

_____

Prom...

_____

_____

_____

Parties...

_____

_____

_____

_____

Graduation...

_____

_____

_____

_____

Graduation gifts...

_____

_____

_____

Jobs...

_____

_____

_____

Mother's Events - etched in our memories!

Your performances, dates and significant notes...

Your first holidays – significant memories and notes…

Daughter's Events - etched in our memories!

My performances, dates and significant notes...

Holidays that I remember and why...

_____

_____

_____

_____

_____

_____

_____

_____

_____

_____

_____

_____

_____

_____

_____

_____

Mother's Events - etched in our memories!

Notes about college...

Where you have decided to go (or went) to college...

_____

_____

Significant clubs, teams or groups that you have chosen to participate in...

_____

_____

_____

The day we moved you into college...

_____

_____

_____

About your roommate(s)...

_____

_____

_____

Things you seem excited about...

_____

_____

_____

_____

Things you seem concerned about...

_____

_____

_____

_____

My prayer for you at college...

_____

_____

_____

_____

Daughter's Events - etched in our memories!

Notes about college...

Where I have decided to go (or went) to college...

_____

_____

Significant clubs, teams or groups that I participate in...

_____

_____

_____

The day my family moved me into college...

_____

_____

_____

About my roommate(s)...

_____

_____

_____

The career that I have chosen is...

_____

_____

_____

Things I am excited about...

_____

_____

_____

Things I am concerned about...

_____

_____

My prayer about college is...

_____

_____

_____

Mother's Events - etched in our memories!

Your wedding day...

How stunningly beautiful you were…

_____

_____

_____

_____

_____

Describe the venue…

_____

_____

_____

_____

What I remember about the rehearsal dinner…

_____

_____

_____

What I remember about the ceremony...

_____

_____

_____

What I remember about the guests....

_____

_____

_____

What I remember about the reception...

_____

_____

_____

What I remember about the way I felt...

_____

_____

_____

_____

_____

Daughter's Events - etched in our memories!
My wedding day...

How lovely you looked as mother of the bride…

_____

_____

_____

_____

How you helped make my wedding day special…

_____

_____

_____

_____

What I remember about the rehearsal dinner…

_____

_____

What I remember about the ceremony...

_____

_____

_____

What I remember about the guests....

_____

_____

_____

What I remember about the reception...

_____

_____

_____

What I remember about the way I felt...

_____

_____

_____

_____

Love is patient, love is kind.
It always protects, always trusts,
always hopes, always perseveres.
Love never fails.

1 Corinthians 13:4, 7-8

14.
Love - such a huge thing for such a small word

Reflections on Love

Mother's Reflections

We are going to share thoughts about love and romance on these pages.

My thoughts about what love is...

_____

_____

_____

_____

_____

_____

_____

_____

_____

_____

_____

_____

_____

My thoughts about what love is not...

Reflections on Love

Daughter's Reflections

We are going to share thoughts about love and romance on these pages.

My thoughts about what love is…

_____

_____

_____

_____

_____

_____

_____

_____

_____

_____

_____

_____

_____

My thoughts about what love is not...

Reflections on Love

Mother's Reflections

What society tells us love is...

_____

_____

_____

_____

_____

_____

_____

_____

_____

_____

_____

_____

_____

_____

_____

Why I disagree or agree with the world's definition of what love is...

Reflections on Love

Daughter's Reflections

What society tells us love is...

_____

_____

_____

_____

_____

_____

_____

_____

_____

_____

_____

_____

_____

_____

_____

_____

Why I disagree or agree with the world's definition of what love is...

Reflections on Love

Mother's Reflections

Books that I have read; movies that I have watched about love, relationships and/or marriage...

Books...

_____

_____

_____

_____

_____

Movies...

_____

_____

_____

_____

_____

People who have helped shape my ideas about love and what they have taught me...

Reflections on Love

Daughter's Reflections

Books that I have read; movies that I have watched about love, relationships and/or marriage…

Books…

_____

_____

_____

_____

_____

Movies…

_____

_____

_____

_____

_____

_____

People who have helped shape my ideas about love and what they have taught me...

Reflections on Love

Mother's Reflections

What I hope you remember most about love...

_____

_____

_____

_____

_____

_____

_____

_____

_____

_____

_____

_____

_____

My advice for you when love is tough...

Reflections on Love

Daughter's Reflections

What I hope I remember most about love…

What I plan to do when love is tough...

Commit to the LORD whatever
you do, and He will establish your plans.

Proverbs 16:3

15.
Achievements and Opportunities - pursuing life

Achievements and Opportunities
Mother's Reflections

My favorite achievement in life so far...

_____

_____

_____

_____

_____

_____

_____

_____

_____

_____

_____

_____

_____

My biggest opportunities in life so far...

Achievements and Opportunities

Daughter's Reflections

My favorite achievement in life so far...

_____

_____

_____

_____

_____

_____

_____

_____

_____

_____

_____

_____

_____

_____

_____

_____

My biggest opportunity in life so far...

Achievements and Opportunities

Mother's Reflections

My favorite thing about being a woman is…

Some things that I still want to accomplish...

Achievements and Opportunities

Daughter's Reflections

My favorite thing about being a girl/woman is…

_____

_____

_____

_____

_____

_____

_____

_____

_____

_____

_____

_____

_____

_____

_____

Some things that I still want to accomplish...

Achievements and Opportunities

Mother's Reflections

Other significant accomplishments...

Other significant opportunities...

Achievements and Opportunities

Daughter's Reflections

Other significant accomplishments...

Other significant opportunities...

Achievements and Opportunities

Mother's Reflections

Something that I would do if I knew that I couldn't fail...

The biggest decision that I have made in my life so far and how it changed things...

Achievements and Opportunities

Daughter's Reflections

Something that I would do if I knew that I couldn't fail…

The biggest decision that I have made in my life so far and how it changed things...

Faith is confidence in what
we hope for and assurance
about what we do not see.

Hebrews 11:1

16.
Inspiration - walk by faith!

Inspiration – Walk by Faith!

Mother's Reflections

What I believe about religion, faith, and God...

What I believe...

_____

_____

_____

_____

_____

_____

_____

_____

_____

_____

_____

_____

_____

Why I believe...

Inspiration – Walk by Faith!

Daughter's Reflections

What I believe about religion, faith, and God…

What I believe...

Why I believe...

_____

_____

_____

_____

_____

_____

_____

_____

_____

_____

_____

_____

_____

_____

_____

_____

_____

_____

_____

_____

_____

Inspiration – Walk by Faith!

Mother's Reflections

From where or whom does my inspiration come?

_____

_____

_____

_____

_____

_____

_____

_____

_____

_____

_____

_____

_____

What are my most significant memories about my faith?

Inspiration – Walk by Faith!

Daughter's Reflections

From where or whom does my inspiration come?

_____

_____

_____

_____

_____

_____

_____

_____

_____

_____

_____

_____

_____

_____

_____

_____

_____

_____

_____

_____

What are my most significant memories about my faith?

Inspiration – Walk by Faith!

Mother's Reflections

What person(s) has inspired me the most in my life? Why?

Whom do I most enjoy inspiring? Why?

Inspiration – Walk by Faith!

Daughter's Reflections

What person(s) has inspired me the most in my life? Why?

Whom do I most enjoy inspiring? Why?

For the happy heart,
life is a continual feast.

Proverbs 15:15

17.
For Fun –
the ways we laugh

For Fun - the ways we laugh

Mother's Reflections

Things you did when you were young that made me smile or laugh...

_____

_____

_____

_____

_____

_____

_____

Things you do or say now that make me smile and laugh...

_____

_____

_____

_____

_____

_____

_____

_____

What I like to do to make you smile...

_____

_____

_____

_____

_____

_____

What I love to do to make you laugh...

_____

_____

_____

_____

_____

_____

_____

_____

_____

For Fun - the ways we laugh

Daughter's Reflections

Things you did when I was young that made me smile or laugh...

_____

_____

_____

_____

_____

Things you do or say now that make me smile and laugh...

_____

_____

_____

_____

_____

_____

_____

_____

What I like to do to make you smile...

_____

_____

_____

_____

_____

_____

What I love to do to make you laugh...

_____

_____

_____

_____

_____

_____

_____

_____

The joy of the LORD
is your strength.

Nehemiah 8:10

18.
Our Space –
all other observations
and feelings

If you would like to share how
this journal has encouraged you
or someone close to you,
we would love to hear from you.

Send us an email:
Publisher@christianartgifts.com